Stock Market Investing for Beginners

Strategies for Long Term Success

Jacob Grant

© **Copyright 2017 by Jacob Grant**

All rights reserved.

The following eBook is reproduced below with the goal of providing information that is as accurate and as reliable as possible. Regardless, purchasing this eBook can be seen as consent to the fact that both the publisher and the author of this book are in no way experts on the topics discussed within, and that any recommendations or suggestions made herein are for entertainment purposes only. Professionals should be consulted as needed before undertaking any of the action endorsed herein.

This declaration is deemed fair and valid by both the American Bar Association and the Committee of Publishers Association and is legally binding throughout the United States.

Furthermore, the transmission, duplication or reproduction of any of the following work, including precise information, will be considered an illegal act, irrespective whether it is done electronically or in print. The legality extends to creating a secondary or tertiary copy of the work or a recorded copy and is only allowed with express written consent of the Publisher. All additional rights are reserved.

The information in the following pages is broadly considered to be a truthful and accurate account of facts, and as such any inattention, use or misuse of the information in question by the reader will render any resulting actions solely under their purview. There are no scenarios in which the publisher or the original author of this work can be in any fashion deemed liable for any hardship or damages that may befall them after undertaking information described herein.

Additionally, the information found on the following pages is intended for informational purposes only and should thus be considered, universal. As befitting its nature, the information presented is without assurance regarding its continued validity or interim quality. Trademarks that mentioned are done without written consent and can in no way be considered an endorsement from the trademark holder.

TABLE OF CONTENTS

Introduction 1

Chapter 1: Start Your Investment with Clear Goals 3

Chapter 2: How to Choose Which Stocks to Invest In ... 10

Chapter 3: How to Purchase Your First Stocks 18

Chapter 4: Different Options for Investing 22

Chapter 5: Different Styles of Stock Trading 32

Chapter 6: Investment Strategies that Work! 38

Chapter 7: The Rules All Investors Should Know Before Getting into the Stock Market 53

Conclusion 61

Description 63

Introduction

Congratulations on downloading your personal copy of *Stock Market Investing for Beginners: Strategies for Long-Term Success*. Thank you for doing so.

The following chapters will discuss some of the many advantages of getting into the stock market. When you want to make your money grow and ensure that you are earning a good income, it is important to find a good investment that will help you to do this. Working with the stock market will help to make this easier than ever and ensures that you are able to make the investment that you deserve.

This guidebook is going to take some time to explore how you would get started with stock market investing. We will start out with some of the basics, such as the different kinds of stock investments you can make. We will then go on to talk about some of the different options that you have, how to decide the amount of risk that you want to take, and even some of the strategies that you can use, based on the risk that you want to take and how much you want to earn, in order to help you to pick the stocks you want and to know when to purchase and sell each one. We will end the guidebook with some tips that all investors can follow to make sure they aren't foiling their own plans.

Stock market investing can be a great way to earn some more money and see your wealth grow; you just need to learn some of the tricks and tips to get started. And with the help of this guidebook, you will be able to learn some of the best strategies out there in order to see some great success with your stock market investment.

There are plenty of books on this subject on the market, thanks again for choosing this one! Every effort was made to ensure it is full of as much useful information as possible. Please enjoy!

Chapter 1: Start Your Investment with Clear Goals

Many people are interested in getting started with some kind of investment in order to grow their money in ways that a normal paycheck just can't do. The investors may have different business plans in place, but they have the same kinds of goals and the same motivation to make money while limiting their risks as much as possible. You may want to help save up for the education for your child or to secure your retirement or you may have simpler goals of affording longer vacations and having some freedom in life.

No matter what your reason for investing is, getting started in the stock market can be the clear choice for many people. It provides you with a great place to put your money and you can choose from a conservative plan to a riskier plan and everywhere in between to see some results. While you will need to take some time to consider which kinds of investments you would like to take, the stock market can provide a great return on investment that everyone can enjoy.

The first thing to understand is a bit of information about the stock market. A stock is a type of security that will give the investor part ownership in a business, as well as some rights to claim ownership of the earnings and the assets of the business. The buyer is going to become a shareholder, and this means that they, as well as the other investors, are going to own that business. Ownership is often determined by how many stocks are available in the company as well as how many stocks you own. The two basic types of stocks include preferred stocks and common stocks.

Common stocks are the ones that will allow you as the buyer the right to go to shareholder meetings and vote on different things with the business, plus you will be able to receive some dividends when the business makes a profit. On the other hand, the preferred stocks are not going to allow the buyer to have any voting rights, but they will have more of a claim on the earnings and the assets of the business compared to some of the common stocks. The preferred stockholder will receive the dividends before a shareholder does and if the business goes through liquidation, they will be the first ones to be compensated.

Easy terms to know

Before we get too far into this process, we need to take a look at some of the easy terms that you should know when it comes to investing in the stock market. Some of the best words to know include:

- Portfolio: this would be the collection of investments that one investor owns.

- Broker: this is the professional who will purchase and sell the different stocks for you and they often work on a commission.

- Dividend: this is going to be the amount of money that you can earn from the stock when the business makes a profit.

- Quotes: this is the information that will

pertain to the latest trading price of the stock.

- Averaging down: this is when you will purchase more of a stock whenever the prices go down to save money.

- Order: this is the bid that you will place when purchasing or selling stocks of a certain amount.

- Execution: this means that one of the orders that you placed has been completed.

- Bear market: this is when the prices of stocks go down on average for a bit of time.

- Bull market: this is the exact opposite of the bear market. This is a longer period of time when there is an increase in your stock prices.

- Day trading: this is a strategy where you are going to buy and sell stocks, all on the same day.

- Margin: this is an account type that is going

to let you borrow some money from your broker in order to make an investment.

- Blue chip stocks: these are the leading companies, and usually large ones, that are in different industries.

- Yield: this is the value of the return of investment that you made. It is often going to be measured by the amount of dividend that you get each year, or each quarter.

- Volatility: this would include all of the changes in the stock price.

- Spread: this is the difference between the bid and the asking price of one stock. It is basically the difference between the amount the seller is willing to sell the stock for and the amount a buyer will pay for it.

How to trade stocks

Most of the stock trading that you will do is done on exchanges, where the sellers and buyers will meet and agree on the right stock price. There are some physical trading floors, but most people do this online. The stock market will help to facilitate this trading and will ensure that both the sellers and the buyers are able to benefit from the investment. The market is also able to reduce the risk of investing so that both parties can get the most benefits.

The prices of stocks are going to change each day thanks to a variety of forces that are in the stock market. If the supply and demand are high for a stock, it can go up, but if the supply goes down, so will the price. The prices of this stock will determine what it is worth and whether or not people will want to purchase the stock. While most of the value for a business is going to be determined by market capitalization, the stock prices are going to matter as well because these will determine the future performance of a company.

The earnings of a particular company should also matter to the investor. This would be the amount of money that the company is making in profits each year and you should be able to find this through the financial journals and reports that the company will provide.

There are quite a few reasons that the stock prices will vary each day so it is hard to list out just one of the reasons. It is going to depend on factors like what the company is doing and if there are any changes there, the economic environment, and so much more. Investors need to realize that the prices of the stocks can be volatile and they do change quite a bit. It does take some time and research to decide which stocks to go with in the beginning to make a profit and sometimes, especially in the beginning, it is possible for you to lose money. Luckily, there are quite a few strategies, and we will discuss a few of them here, that you are able to use to limit some of the risks that you are taking.

Chapter 2: How to Choose Which Stocks to Invest In

With all of the different types of stocks that we are able to choose from, it can seem confusing to know where to start. The important first step is that you should never rush into picking out a stock just because you think it looks good or you don't understand how it works. You need to perform a good analysis to select the right stock because this helps you to get into the right frame of mind and to ask the hard questions to get good companies.

If you already have a list of companies you would like to consider, go to their website and see if there is some information there that relates to their stocks. Look at their financial reports too because this helps you to see how well the company is doing on the market. When you get a good understanding of the financial information about your company, you are more likely to make a good investment.

Of course, you want to make sure that you choose an investment that will do well if you want to make money. This helps your peace of mind so that you know the investment will not go to waste and you can get a return that is worth your time. Some of the factors that you should look for when determining how well a company is doing include:

- The profit margin of that company.
- The return on equity for that company.
- The past performance as well as the expected growth.
- The debts that the company currently has.
- The debt to equity ratio. This means that you would take the debt of the company and divide it by the equity of the shareholders. If this is a low number, it is a safer investment.

What should I look for inside a company?

As a beginner, you may be unsure of which kinds of companies you should work with when it comes to picking out the right investment. While some beginners are going to rush into the market without thinking it through, it is important to stop and look at many aspects of the company, from their performance to their management and everywhere in between. Some of the factors that you should consider include:

Business management

This is one of the most important factors because the management of the business will determine how well it does in the future. While you probably won't be able to go and meet with the business management, there are a few signs to look for. The return on equity and how much income the shareholders earn each year can really show you how well the business is using its money. If you notice that the return on equity ends up being at least 5 percent or higher, this one is a pretty safe investment.

Stocks from a good business sector

Choosing the business industry that you want to

invest in is important. There are some industries that are going to do better than others and some that are more volatile. You can choose to spread out your money and invest it into more than one industry as well to grow your portfolio. When you are ready to diversify your portfolio, which can be great for reducing the risk of your investment, you should look for some stocks that are from leading industries get started on. If you invested in an industry that is not doing that well, you can always take the money out and restart somewhere else.

Growing profits:

You will want to invest in companies that are already making profits. A company that shows growing profits can be even better. You should start with companies that have steady share growth that is at least 5 percent. This helps to keep your investment safe when you are first getting started and can help you to get some money every year that you are investing with the company.

The company size

You will find that smaller companies are going to be riskier to invest in compared to some of the big ones. The bigger companies have had more time to establish themselves so it is harder for tough economic times or other things to bring them out. Many beginners start with this and can take on more of the risk when they get a chance to be in the market longer and know how to read it better. It is also a bad idea to go with penny stocks as a beginner because they can be really risky. The big businesses are a great way to give you a good return each year ad can be safer.

Manageable debt

While there are many companies that have debts, it is the way that they manage it, and how much they have, that can make or break the company. You should check out how much debt the company has, especially when compared with how much profit they bring in. If the company has too much in debt, they are going to end up paying you less because they have to pay things off and if they keep taking on that debt, they may go under with their shareholders going down as well. A rate of .5 for the debt per capital ratio is the healthiest to go with.

Dividend Payments

Companies that are able to return a part of their profits to the investors are the ones who will be the best to go with since you will make money with them. They are able to properly manage their money in a way that not only are they able to pay off their debts, pay their workers, and still have enough to pay their investors as well. You should also consider the amount of dividend payment that the company is able to give to their investors. One that is at least 2 percent is a great place to start so see if your company is able to do this amount. dividends are additional financial benefits that all investors need to consider when they are investing their money and this is where you will be able to determine your return on investment, so of course, it makes sense to try and get it to be as high as possible.

Stocks with enough liquidity

This is important because you want to make sure that you are able to get something when you sell the stock. The ones that are considered liquid are the stocks that you are easily able to sell because there are some buyers for it. If you decide for some reason that you want to get out of the stock market, you want it to be liquid enough that you are able to sell it later. There are a few stocks that are not that liquid and it is going to be a lot of work to try to sell them, which can cost you a lot of money if the market does go down at some time. Consider going with some stocks that will allow you to sell them fast if you find that the need does arise.

As you can see, you will need to take the time to really look at all of the aspects of a company to see if it is going to be a good investment to help you out. you should take a look at all of these aspects when it comes to which companies you would like to invest in because it will help you to know if it is healthy or if there are some issues that will arise with your earnings. If you can do this complete analysis, it is going to be much easier or you to get the return on investment that you want.

Chapter 3: How to Purchase Your First Stocks

For a beginner, the most challenging step is learning how to purchase one of your first stocks. They are not used to taking these risks and can it make them feel a little nervous about all of this. You may know some of the basics, but you will need to understand some of the different methods that you can use in order to get your stocks purchased and start working with the investment. There are three main options that you can work with when deciding to purchase your first stocks including:

Using a broker

This is one of the most common methods that you can purchase a stock. Brokers can take over some of the hard work for you, but help to chase stocks and even selling them for you. As a beginner in this industry, you can definitely benefit from some of the knowledge and support that you get from your broker while you learn how to operate and manage your very own account.

There are two main types of brokers you can go with. The full-service broker is the one who will be responsible for managing your account and it usually costs a bit more for this service. These used to be the only kinds of brokers available, but since some people decide to manage their own accounts, that has changed. If you want to have someone walk you through the process or you are nervous about doing it on your own, hiring a full-service broker is the way to go.

There are also discount brokers. These are often less expensive, which makes them a little more popular and readily available, but you do need to remember that you will have to put in some of the work on your own. You will be the one to decide how to work with the stocks, when to purchase them and when to sell them, but you are able to get started for a much lower price.

Working with dividends reinvestment plans

This is a plan where you will work with an individual company. This company will allow you to take the money that you earn in dividends each year and place them into purchasing more stocks. This is a good way to invest if you are only able to start out with a small amount of money because you can keep reinvesting what you have made. This one does take a little bit to earn a good amount of money, but if you are short on money to get started with or you are looking for long-term gains, this would be a good way to grow that smaller investment without all the risk.

Direct investment plans

With this one, you would avoid going through a broker to make the purchases at all. You would find an individual company that you want to work with, and then instead of going through a broker or a brokerage company, you would just keep purchasing the stocks directly from that company. This will come with a small fee, but there are some times when it can save you money.

All of these can be great methods to help you to get into the stock market and working with the company that you want in order to make some money. You may start out with just a little bit of money, you may start out with a broker doing most of the work for you, or you may start out with something quite a bit different. But these are options that you can do in order to finally get into the investing of stock markets and seeing a good return on your investment.

Chapter 4: Different Options for Investing

When it comes to picking out the niche that you want to invest in, there are quite a few options that you are able to choose from. It is often going to depend on the amount of money that you would like to make and even the risk that you are willing to take overall. Even with having a good research plan in place, many investors still need to be a bit skeptical about the investment that they are making because there is a degree of risk in all of them. Here we are going to look at some of the main niches and options that you can use when it comes to investing in stocks.

Investing in dividend stocks

If your investment strategy is all about going for the long term, you are going to really benefit from a wide choice of stocks that you can purchase. You will have a lot of choices for the companies you want to work with and if you are good at picking out stocks, you can enjoy dividend income for the long term with very little work on your part.

Keep in mind that not all of the stocks that you see are going to be dividends so you will need to look around to make sure that you are finding the right ones. First, you need to understand how the stock is going to yield a dividend ad then you can pick out the one that you should work with. screening a few companies and figuring out if they make profits, as well as how much they actually retain, can help you to pick out a stock that will do a great job. The good news is that you are able to look at the financial statements of most companies so you can see which ones are the dividend achievers.

Once you have a good list of the stocks that pay dividends, you will want to ensure that you are picking the ones that are the highest quality. Some of the things that you can look for to determine if the dividend stock is a good one include:

- The company has dividend payments that are uninterrupted. You should look back as far as you can to see if there is ever a time when the dividends are missing.
- Look out for how high the return on equity is. If you look at the average over five years, it should be around 15 to 20 percent.

- Look for rising earnings and rising sales for each share.

- Look for the growth in dividends. The best companies are going to have a growth of this dividend being at least 5 percent over the past ten years.

Looking for the answers of these will help you to rank the companies that you would like to work with. you can then figure out which one is going to come out the winner and then pick that to start out your investment.

Investing in foreign stocks

Some experienced investors like to work with foreign stocks, but this can be a good place for you to enter as well if you are careful with your research and don't rush in. foreign companies can be quite promising and some investors are going to get really returns on their investment. But it is important to remember that these foreign companies do have a higher risk that you should not ignore. There is also the challenge of trying to figure out what company is the best one for you to invest in, which takes a lot of research on your side. There are still a few benefits of going with these foreign stocks, despite some of the extra risks, including:

Foreign stocks are going to represent an added opportunity for investing. You may find that it is hard to find the local company that you want to work with, but depending on what you are looking for, you may be able to find that company internationally.

It helps with diversifying. You need to make sure that you are spreading out the risks that come with your investment. One way to do this is to use more than one company when you are investing. Adding in some foreign stocks can make this easier.

Of course, it is important to not overlook some of the risks that come with these foreign stocks. There are some big risks that come from these including from the exchange rate. Your return on the stock could end up catering for currency exchange rates from the currency of that country over to your own. The economy of another country, not the economy of yours, will determine how much you are able to earn or lose. You should probably be careful when it comes to investing in countries that are suffering from social and political issues.

However, even though there are some bigger risks, in the long run, it can also mean that you will have more rewards when you reach the end. If you can find a good company overseas to work with overseas, you can make a big return on your investment.

Working with penny stocks

Another option that you can choose is to work in penny stocks. These are a type of stock that will have some smaller share prices, which often makes it easier for others to get into the stock market to get started, even if they don't have a ton of money to invest. Investors like this option because it doesn't cost them as much as other options. There are some benefits and even disadvantages to this method. One advantage is that they are more affordable so you will not have to come up with a large amount of money to just get started.

However, it also has some bad issues with the value of the stock. If there are any kinds of negative movements in the stock, even if they are just a little bit, they are going to make a huge impact on the penny stocks and even the return that you can get overall. Many of the trades that come with penny stocks are also not going to be regulated, unlike the other investment types, so you will also have that risk as well. If you are interested in investing in these penny stocks, there are a few guidelines that you are able to follow including:

- Always ready the warnings that are provided by the regulators.
- Do your own background check on the company.
- Make sure that the penny stock is really what you want to work with.
- Make sure that you understand how much disclosure the company is giving you and if this is really the best method to use.

Each of the options above is going to provide you with varying amounts of risk factors to consider and other options that will help you to make the right decisions for yourself. The great thing about stock market investing though is that you are able to work on many different types of stocks, rather than just being stuck with one option when picking out your investment type.

Chapter 5: Different Styles of Stock Trading

So, stock trading is basically going to entail selling and buying of stocks in order to make more returns compared to an investor who is going to purchase a stock and then hold onto it for their future benefit. The traders are going to work to make more profits, or income, from the work that they do and if it is done right, they could make an income each day with this work. As a trader, if you decide to go with this option, you are going to aim at purchase a stock low and then selling it high so that they can make their income on this difference. The period of trading is usually going to be short and will vary based on your personal style.

When you want to pick out a style of trading, there are going to be a few options that you can pick from. The four main trading styles that most traders are going to pick from includes:

Position trading

This is one of the longest trading periods. These can take a few months and even up to a few years, which allows the trader some more time to watch the trends inside o the market before they have to make their decisions to purchase or to sell. This one is more skewed towards an investment option, but they are open to both long-term as well as short-term strategies, unlike those who are sticking with the long-term trades. Position traders will consistently look at weekly and monthly charts to help them to make their decisions for trading. They will not take a look at the short-term price changes, unlike some other stock traders, in order to help them earn the most from their investments.

Day trading:

With this trading style, you are going to enter into a new trade and then sell on the same day. They will never hold onto their stocks overnight so once the market closes. The trader will have to stop at whatever they have at the end of the day. These day traders are going to look often at technical analysis in order to figure out the last few days, as well as the trends, that go up with the stocks that they want to purchase and trade.

This one is not going to bring about a lot of profit because of the small amount of time that they are trading in and there are not often significant changes that happen in just a few hours. What they are capitalizing on with this one are the small as well as the frequent profits that they will get with day trading. This is a good one to do for a living for a replacement income because they can make some good money when spread out each day and you do need to have a lot of time to monitor them.

Swing trading

This is a trading style where you will hold onto the stocks for up to a few weeks. These traders are going to look onto the short-term fluctuations of the prices in order to get a profitable trade. They will also spend some time on a technical analysis because it helps them to see the changes that will possibly occur with the stock prices. The fundamentals of a company are not going to be that important because the swing trader will just leave the trade when they are all done with their goals. This is a good one if you want to make some profits quickly, but you don't have a lot of time to watch the stock market all day long.

Scalp trading

This one is related to day trading, but it is a little more active because you are going to do a lot of purchasing and selling of these stocks throughout the day. The day to day changes that come with stock prices is going to become your main focus with this option. They are going to purchase a stock when it is low and then try to sell it when the fluctuations of the day bring it up. These profits are pretty low, usually just a few dollars each, but when you do quite a few of these each day, it can add up.

Choosing your trading style

Now that we have talked about a few of the options that you can use, it is time to pick out your own personal trading style. Picking out a good trading style can be hard, but you first need to make sure that you know what you would like to get out of the stock market. There are a few factors that you can consider including:

- The size of your account
- How much time you will be able to devote to your trades.
- Your experience level when it comes to trading
- Your tolerance for risk
- Your own personality.

For the most part, the amount of time that you would like to spend on trading will take up a big consideration when you are picking out the trading style that you would like to go with. For example, if your schedule is busy and you are only able to give a few hours each week to monitoring your stock charts, you will probably want to be a position trader. On the other hand, if you are able to spend a lot of time looking over the charts and picking the right options for you, going with day trading or scalp trading is better. Over time, you may even want to diversify your portfolio a bit more and will find that having more than one of these investment styles can bring in the most money for your needs.

Chapter 6: Investment Strategies that Work!

There are several different strategies that you are able to use when you first get started in the stock market. You are able to use any of these that you would like, just make sure that you understand the risk and the reward with each of them and then stick with the same strategy rather than skipping around the whole time. Here we are going to look at some of the most common investment strategies that you are able to use to see great results in stock market investing.

Fundamental analysis

This is a pretty straightforward option but it will take some research and a little bit of time to complete. The goal is to analyze the company that you want to work and invest with in order to find the intrinsic value of the company. Basically, the intrinsic value is a term for how much you think the stock is worth compared to the currently traded value of the company on the market. If you find that the intrinsic value is going to be higher than the current price of the company, it would make sense for you to purchase the stock based on this strategy because the stock is likely to go up and you can make some good money with a bit of waiting.

Although there are some different methods that you can use in order to find the intrinsic value, the premise is pretty similar with all of them. You want to find the worth of the company and this is going to be the sum of its discounted cash flows. What this means is that the company is worth all of the future profits added together and then these future profits are going to be discounted to account for the time value, or the force of which the $1 you receive today is going to be worth less than it was today.

The idea with the intrinsic value equaling the future profits will make sense when you think about how the business should provide some value for the owners. If you own a small business, its worth will be all the money that you are able to take from the company each year. And you can only take something from the company if there is something left after debts, salaries, supplies, and so much more. A business is going to be all about your profits, or the revenue minus the expenses and figuring all of this out can help you to find the intrinsic value.

In order to come up with the numbers that you want with this, you just need to do a little bit of research. Having a good look at the financial report of the company and checking out some of the news about them and the numbers that come around with this company. But with a bit of research, you will find that you can figure out the intrinsic value and pick the right companies.

Value investing

This is one of the most popular stock-picking

methods. The person who picks value investing is going to look for some stocks that have a lot of strong fundamentals, such as book value, cash flow, dividends, and earnings. Then they will compare the price that the stocks are being sold at and see how it compares to these fundamentals. The value investor is going to seek some companies that seem to be undervalued based on their fundamentals because they will be able to get these stocks at a good price and at some point, the stocks have the potential to increase to market value and they will make a great profit.

Before looking at this one, we need to understand there is a difference between value investing and junk stocks. There are some stocks that are at a low price because they are not worth very much money. They may have bad management, not be worth much, or have way too much debt and aren't going to make you any money at all. The value stocks are ones that have a strong earning potential, low debt, and pay good dividends, but because of how the market is working or something else, the stock is being offered for a good price. The value stock is going to go up at some point because it is a strong company, and you can make money while the junk stocks will never go up, probably will go down, because something is wrong with the company.

With value investing, you are going to buy the business rather than the stock. They are going to take a look at how the company runs and decide if they want to invest in the company, rather than looking at the stock. They won't look at any of the external factors that affect the company, such as a bad economy, but they are going to focus on the underlying worth of the company and see if it may go back up at some time.

Some people don't like this method because they feel that most stocks are at the price that they deserve and they think it is dangerous to not look at the price at all. Others find that they are able to find some great deals on a company by looking more at the way that it is managed, rather than watching all of the different factors that are going on around it that are beyond its control.

CAN SLIM

The next one we are going to talk about is the CAN SLIM philosophy that will take a bit more work but is an acronym that is going to stand for a great strategy that will help you to make some good choices when it comes to the stocks that you choose to purchase. The best thing about going with this option is that there is some great evidence about how this will work. Let's take a look at how this one is going to work:

C = Current Earnings

This one is going to look at the current earnings o the company. You will want to check out the earnings in the recent quarter for the company and then compare them to this same quarter from the year before. You should see that the earnings are higher than they were in the year before. The growth amount is debatable, but the system suggests that the growth is somewhere between 18 and 20 percent. You do need to do a bit of digging on here though because some companies will try to manipulate the earnings. Check out some of the earnings of other companies to see if the numbers seem realistic or not.

A = Annual earnings

This one is also going to take a look at the annual earnings growth. You should be able to look over the past five years for a company and see that they are seeing growth over all of them. You should look for an annual earnings growth that is somewhere between 25 and 50 percent over this time.

N = New

The third criteria are that there has been some change in the company, which can often be necessary in order to help it become successful.

This could be a new product, a new high in the stock price, a new market, or even new people on the management team. Look for some of these things to see if a company is good for you to go with.

S = Supply and Demand

This one is going to stand for supply and demand, which is going to refer to a law that will govern all of the activities that happen in the market. With this one, when all other things are equal inside of the market, it is going to be easier for a smaller firm, with a smaller number of shares outstanding, to show more gains. The reasoning is that a larger company will require more demand compared to a smaller company in order to demonstrate the same kinds of gains.

Lim = Leader

For this part of the process, it is going to take a look between the leaders and the laggards and see if this helps you to make some decisions. No matter what industry you are in, there are always going to be some companies that are the leaders, the ones that will provide their shareholders with some great leads, and then there are those that are going to lag behind, and won't provide you with all that great of a return. Your goal is to pick the leaders so that you are able to find ones that provide you with a great return on the investment.

I = Institutional Sponsorship

This one is going to help you to see the benefits of having some kind of institutional sponsorship. Basically, the idea o this one is that a company doesn't have an institutional sponsorship, it means that the thousands of institutional money managers passed over the company for some reason. To pick out a stock that is going to do well for you, you need to have one that contains at least three, but preferably more, institutional owners.

On the other hand, you do need to be careful when the company is owned primarily by institutions. It is possible for a company to be too institutionally owned and when this happens, it is already too late for you to get into the company and it could end up with a big sell-off on the company. Look for it to have a few of these around, but be careful if there are too many.

M = Market direction

The final criteria that need to be met here is market direction. When you are picking out some new stocks, it is important to remember that you need to check out the market and understand whether it is a bull or a bear market. If you aren't able to understand the market direction right now, you may end up investing against the current trend, and this can compromise your gains or even how much you lose quite a bit. Before getting into this option, you will need to get a good understanding of which way the market is working so that you can work on picking out the right stocks.

You will be able to work on this option in order to look at may different parts when it comes to picking out the stocks that you want to work with. It does take some time, but there are many studies that show how great this option can be when it comes to helping you to make a good return on your investment compared to the others, you just need to learn how to make it work.

Income Investing

With income investing, you are going to try and pick companies that will provide you with a pretty steady stream of income, but it is pretty simple and straightforward when it comes to investing. When investors think of a steady income, they will pick out some options like bonds and fixed income securities. Of course, if you pick out a good stock, you can also use some stocks in order to end up with a steady income stream each quarter.

Now with this one, you will need to pick out a stock that makes a good dividend to you. The average yield for many of the stocks on the exchange are going to make about three percent, but if you are trying to earn an income on this, you will want to make at least 6 percent to make it worth your time. This means that you need to be able to go through and find some great stocks that give a higher dividend compared to some others.

In addition to finding a good stock that will produce a predictable and steady stream of money over a long period of time, you will also need to take a look at the dividend policy. The income investor needs to determine whether one of the companies they are considering will be able to continue on with these dividends into the future. If the company has recently increased the number of dividends, you need to take a look at that decision and decide if they will be able to keep going with that. If you see that there was a large increase that happened over just a year or two, it may end up being something that is overly optimistic and it is not a good one to stick with. To make this work, you need to be able to look over the long term of the company and see that it has been paying large dividends for a long time. If the company has been doing this for a long time, it is likely to keep on doing it in the future.

Dogs of the Dow

Another option that you can choose is the Dogs of the Dow. This is a simple approach, which is why some beginners like to go with it, but you have to stick with it for the long term rather than something that is short term. With this one, you will take a look at the 30 companies that are in the Dow Jones Industrial Average (DIJA) and then pick the ten that are performing the best. Then at the end of the year, you will look at the 30 that are there again, pick the top ten, and readjust the portfolio for any of the ones that changed in that year.

This means that each year you are going to get rid of a few of these stocks every year and replace them because these stocks have fallen out of the top ten or because they are removed from the DIJA.

Now, this is not going to be full proof. The theory is going over the assumption that what worked during the 20th century is going to continue on for the 21st century, but because it is a simple one to go with, a lot of beginner investors will like to go with. You will just need to watch the DIJA every year and pick out the one that is doing the best and then change them out each year if needed.

Often this is the one picked just because it is simple. You will not have to look through your or watch all of the charts or other things when you are busy. You will need to take some time to look through the information at the beginning of the year to see which stocks you need to change or talk to your brokcr to see which ones they will change for you. This is a long term investment that is great for keeping your investment secure and ensuring that you get a good income in the process.

There are many great strategies that you can work with that will make it easier for you to get some great results. The trick here is to find the one that is going to help you to work with the style that you want. You do need to be careful about the one that you pick because it is best to stick with just one, rather than trying to switch around all of the time and having issues when this occurs. But overall you can do well with any of these strategies and it often depends on the one that works the best for you.

Chapter 7: The Rules All Investors Should Know Before Getting into the Stock Market

While everyone who gets into the stock market will have a different strategy that they want to use and different ways that they are going to do things, it is important to realize that there are a few rules that you are able to follow to help out. Some beginners choose to go away from these rules, but they often run into a lot of trouble along the way. They will get in their own way, going against some of their own plans, and end up running into a lot of issues in the meantime. Some of the rules that any stock market investor can consider includes:

Avoid going with the crowd mentality

There are a lot of people who rely on their neighbors, friends, and other people in their lives in order to make some important decisions about their stock picks. But you need to realize that most of these people either know nothing about the stock market or they want you to react in a certain manner because it will help their own stocks make money. When you go with the crowd mentality and start taking advice from lots of different people, you will also find there is the issue with not being able to think about things clearly.

As an investor in the stock market, you need to make sure that you are not following along with the decisions of other people. You should always be afraid when others are acting greedy for a stock, but then act greedy when others are being afraid of that stock. This will serve you much better because often when lots of people go after one stock, it ends up backfiring on them all because prices get too high while dividends are low.

Pick an investment approach and stick with it

There are many great strategies that you are able to use when you get into the stock market, but the trick is to pick one and stick with it. One of the reasons that many beginners are going to fail is because they don't have any discipline. You need to find a system that works for you and then put your money into the right shares, and holding onto the investments right amount of time, based on the strategy that you have picked. How are you supposed to see results if you are always switching things around all of the time?

As a beginner, you may be tempted to rush into things in order to make some good money, but when you do this, you are not able to think things through well. You should also be careful about trying to recover any of the losses that you had in the past. The best thing that you can have when you are working in the stock market is patience. You should also watch out for your long-term goals, rather than worry so much about what happens from day to day.

Don't try to time the market

Trying to time how the stock market works is one of the reasons that a lot of beginners in the stock market end up losing a lot of their money each day. It is pretty much impossible to catch on to the tops and the bottoms of their stock and trying to do this can make it really frustrating when things don't go your way. The best thing that you can do is to stick with the trading style that you picked and then use those to pick your trading times, and you will be fine.

There are going to be some financial planners who will insist that this method of timing the stock market is going to backfire on the investor, and these are the ones that you should follow. The investor who tries to outsmart the stock market is the one who is going to lose all of their money and not do well in stock market investing. The stock market is able to change in just a few seconds, which makes timing almost impossible, so don't even try it.

Only invest the surplus funds

One thing that you should get used to when starting in the stock market is that you need to only invest the money that you are able to afford to lose. There are going to be times when the market goes down and you can't predict all of this. But this is going to end up being a hard thing to handle if you put too much money or more money than you can afford to lose. You should never try to invest all of the money that you hope to gain in the beginning because if you end up losing out, your financial position can be losing.

You will find over time that the stock market is not that stable, which is one of the main reasons that you should never try to use more funds than you are able to lose. Of course, you are not always going to lose, but having a plan in place in case you do lose can help to limit those risks and keeps you ready to keep on going whether you lose or not.

Never let the emotions get in the way

When the emotions start to get in the way, it is going to be really hard to think clearly about the decisions that you need to make. Your ability to be able to control your emotions will help you to keep the stock market investment as safe as possible. There are many times someone is going to become emotional about their investment, but when these emotions get in the way, they will cause you to make irrational decisions, and depending on which decision you make, they could cost you a big part, or all, of your investment.

The two emotions that are associated with investing in the stock market include greed and fear. Sometimes you will be faced with a possibility of making a lot of money ad that urges to become rich quickly is really hard for a lot of people to resist. But what you have to remember is that while there are times when you could make a lot of money, there is also something attached to it that makes it really risky. Your chances of losing money in these situations are at least as high, if not higher, than your chance of becoming rich.

Greed is the reason that a lot of investors are going to speculate and then they end up purchasing some shares of companies that they don't know about or even they will create a big position without thinking twice about the risks that are involved, especially when it comes to a bull market. Once the market reverses, you will end up losing a lot of money. And then with a bear market, you will sell the shares out of fear and you will lose a lot of money in the process as well. As you can see, the emotions get into the way with both of these and if you are able to think through your decisions a little bit better, you can save your investment with smart decisions, rather than just relying on your emotions.

Keep your expectations realistic

While it is always a good thing to hope for the best in your stock market investment, but you should be realistic about the things that you hope to achieve. If you go with expectations that are out of lie with reality, you will find that it will push you to make some irrational decisions in the hopes of meeting up with these expectations. You should spend some time to think about all of the outcomes that are possible with the stock market and be ready for them just in case so that you can avoid some of the issues with emotional trading.

Yes, there are going to be times when you can make a lot of money on your investment, for example, but this is not always going to be how things go, no matter how good you are at investing. There are going to be times when you will lose out and if you are able to recognize this, you are going to be more realistic about the risks that you take and you will be more careful with the decisions that you make.

Even if you are a beginner in the stock market, there are a lot of things that you have to get used to and you have to be careful about the decisions that you make. But if you are able to follow some of the simple steps that are in this chapter and follow a few of the ideas and rules, you will find that you are less likely to fail and you will see the results that you want.

Conclusion

Thank for making it through to the end of *Stock Market Investing for Beginners: Strategies for Long-Term Success*. Let's hope it was informative and able to provide you with all of the tools you need to achieve your goals of

The next step is to decide which niche you would like to go with and the strategy that you want to go with in order to be successful. This helps you to figure out what you would like to do with the stock market investment and will ensure that you are able to make some money with this option.

This guidebook will take some time to look over some of the basics that you need to know in order to get started in stock market investing. We spent some time looking at some of the basics of the stock market and which options you are able to go with depending on the amount of time that you are able to work in the stock market, how much risk you would like to take, and so much more. We also spend some time talking about the strategies that you can use on the stock market and the simple rules that you should follow in order to really see some great results.

The stock market is a great way to make your money work for you when you decide to invest, but you should make sure that you have a plan in place and understand some of your own risks. When you are ready to get started with your own stock market investment, make sure to read through this guidebook and learn just how to get started.

Finally, if you found this book useful in any way, a review on Amazon is always appreciated!

Description

When it comes to picking out a new investment strategy, there are many industries that you can get into. One of the most efficient methods, and one that can provide you with a lot of options, includes the stock market. For beginners, working in the stock market can be difficult, but with the help of this guidebook, you will be able to learn all the best tips and make this investment work for you.

Some of the things that we are going to learn about stock market investing in this guidebook include:

- How to start your investment with some clear goals
- How to choose which stocks you want to invest in
- How to purchase your first stocks
- Some of the different options you have for investing.
- The different styles of stock trading

- Investment strategies that work!
- The rules all investors should know before they get into the stock market

When you are ready to get your money to go to work for you, it is time to get into stock market investing. This guidebook is going to give you all of the tips and information that you need in order to go from beginner to professional in the stock market.

www.ingramcontent.com/pod-product-compliance
Lightning Source LLC
Chambersburg PA
CBHW061205180526
45170CB00002B/968